A CINEMATIC HISTORY of GANGSTERS & DETECTIVES

MARK WILSHIN

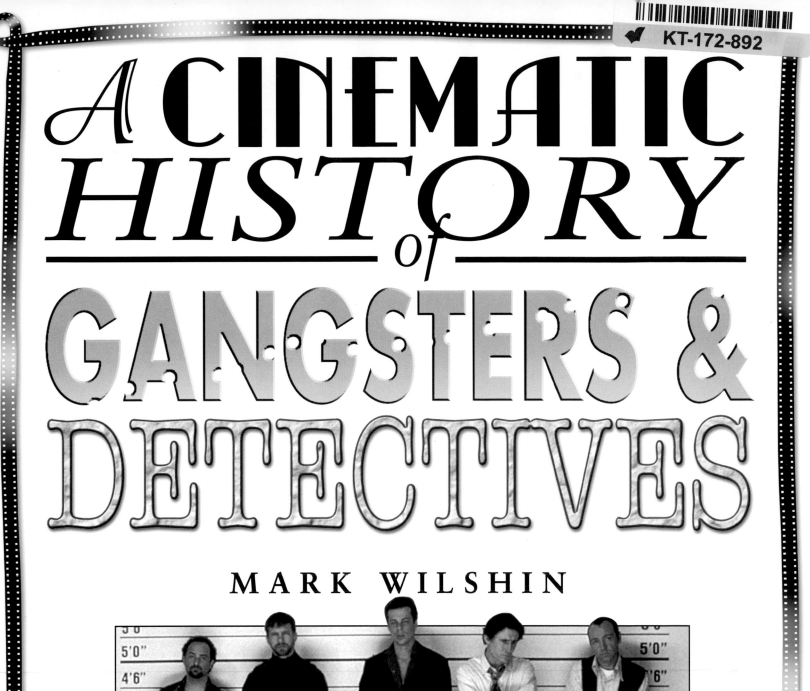

CONTENTS

A CINEMATIC HISTORY of GANGSTERS & DETECTIVES

www.raintreepublishers.co.uk
Visit our website to find out more information about
Raintree books.

To order:
☎ Phone 44 (0) 1865 888113
📄 Send a fax to 44 (0) 1865 314091
💻 Visit the Raintree bookshop at
www.raintreepublishers.co.uk to browse our
catalogue and order online.

A CINEMATIC HISTORY OF GANGSTERS & DETECTIVES
was produced by

David West 🯅 Children's Books

7 Princeton Court
55 Felsham Road
London SW15 1AZ

Designer: Gary Jeffrey
Editor: Rowan Lawton
Picture Research: Gail Bushnell

First published in Great Britain by
Raintree, Halley Court, Jordan Hill, Oxford OX2
8EJ, part of Harcourt Education. Raintree is a
registered trademark of Harcourt Education Ltd.

08 07 06 05
10 9 8 7 6 5 4 3 2 1

ISBN 1 844 21082 0

British Library Cataloguing in Publication Data

Wilshin, Mark
A cinematic history of gangters and detectives
1.Gangster films - History and criticism - Juvenile
    literature 2.Detective and mystery films - History
    and criticism - Juvenile literature
I.Title
791.4'36556

Printed and bound in China

PHOTO CREDITS :

Abbreviations: t-top, m-middle, b-bottom, r-right,
l-left, c-centre.

cover, t, POLYGRAM / SPELLING / THE KOBAL COLLECTION, c,
PARAMOUNT / THE KOBAL COLLECTION, r, WARNER BROS / FIRST
NATIONAL / THE KOBAL COLLECTION; 3, Photo By
C.20THC.FOX/EVERETT / REX FEATURES; 4l, UNITED ARTISTS / THE
KOBAL COLLECTION, 4r, Photo By EVERETT COLLECTION / REX
FEATURES; 5, Photo By EVERETT COLLECTION / REX FEATURES; 6t, Photo
By EVERETT COLLECTION / REX FEATURES, 6b, NERO / THE KOBAL
COLLECTION; 7t, Photo By EVERETT COLLECTION / REX FEATURES, 7c,
ASSOCIATED BRITISH / THE KOBAL COLLECTION, 7b, Photo By REX
FEATURES; 8t, Photo By SNAP / REX FEATURES, 8b, Photo By EVERETT
COLLECTION / REX FEATURES; 9l, Photo By EVERETT COLLECTION / REX
FEATURES, 9c, ALLIED ARTISTS / THE KOBAL COLLECTION9b, THE
KOBAL COLLECTION; 10t, LUX/VIDES/GALATEA / THE KOBAL
COLLECTION, 10l, LADD COMPANY/WARNER BROS / THE KOBAL
COLLECTION, 10r, Roger Viollet / REX FEATURES; 11t, WARNER BROS /
THE KOBAL COLLECTION, 11b, UNIVERSAL / THE KOBAL COLLECTION /
GOLDMAN, LOUIS; 12t, TAPLIN-PERRY-SCORSESE / THE KOBAL
COLLECTION, 12r, Photo By EVERETT COLLECTION / REX FEATURES, 12l,
RIGHT VISION/BANDAI / THE KOBAL COLLECTION; 13t, MILESTONE /
THE KOBAL COLLECTION, 13c, MIRAMAX/BUENA VISTA / THE KOBAL
COLLECTION, 13b, BASIC PICTURES/MEDIA ASIA FILMS LTD / THE
KOBAL COLLECTION; 14l, UNITED ARTISTS / THE KOBAL COLLECTION,
14r, 14b, Photo By REX FEATURES; 15r, SOLAR/FIRST ARTISTS/NATIONAL
GENERAL / THE KOBAL COLLECTION, 15b, WARNER BROS / THE KOBAL
COLLECTION / BALDWIN, SIDNEY; 16t, Photo By SNAP / REX FEATURES,
16l, Photo By C.WARNER BR/EVERETT / REX FEATURES, 16r, Photo By REX
FEATURES; 17t, Photo By EVERETT COLLECTION / REX FEATURES, 17l,
Photo By EVERETT COLLECTION / REX FEATURES, 17r, WARNER BROS /
THE KOBAL COLLECTION / MARSHAK, BOB; 18t, PARAMOUNT / THE
KOBAL COLLECTION, 18l, A BAND APART/MIRAMAX / THE KOBAL
COLLECTION, 18r, Photo By EVERETT COLLECTION / REX FEATURES; 19t,
GAUMONT/CECCHI GORI/TIGER / THE KOBAL COLLECTION, 19c,
HOLLYWOOD PICTURES / THE KOBAL COLLECTION / GORDON,
MELINDA SUE, 19b, A BAND APART/MIRAMAX / THE KOBAL
COLLECTION / COOPER, ANDREW; 20t, Photo By EVERETT COLLECTION
/ REX FEATURES, 20b, Photo By C.20THC.FOX/EVERETT / REX FEATURES;
21t, THE KOBAL COLLECTION, 21r, Photo By EVERETT COLLECTION /
REX FEATURES, 21b, MONARCHY/REGENCY / THE KOBAL COLLECTION
/ CONNOR, FRANK; 22t, Photo By SNAP / REX FEATURES, 22l, ORION /
THE KOBAL COLLECTION, 22r, Photo By EVERETT COLLECTION / REX
FEATURES, 22b, UNITED ARTISTS / THE KOBAL COLLECTION /
ZUCKERMAN, ROBERT; 23t, Photo By REX FEATURES, 23b,
NARC/CUTTING EDGE/CRUISE-WAGNER / THE KOBAL COLLECTION /
COURTNEY, MICHAEL; 24r, UNITED ARTISTS / THE KOBAL COLLECTION,
24b, WARNER BROS / THE KOBAL COLLECTION; 25r, UA/LIONS GATE /
THE KOBAL COLLECTION, 25l, POLYGRAM/WORKING TITLE / THE
KOBAL COLLECTION / MORTON, MERRICK, 25b, Photo By SNAP / REX
FEATURES; 26r, Photo By SNAP / Rex Features, 26l, UNIVERSAL / THE KOBAL
COLLECTION, 26b, UNITED ARTISTS / THE KOBAL COLLECTION; 27l,
MGM / THE KOBAL COLLECTION, 27r, EMI / THE KOBAL COLLECTION;
28r, Photo By C.COLUMBIA/EVERETT / REX FEATURES, 28b, UNIVERSAL /
THE KOBAL COLLECTION, 29l, UNIVERSAL / THE KOBAL COLLECTION /
CARUSO, PHILLIP, 29r, TOUCHSTONE / THE KOBAL COLLECTION; 30t,
PARAMOUNT / THE KOBAL COLLECTION

Every effort has been made to contact copyright
holders of any material reproduced in this book.
Any omissions will be rectified in subsequent
printings if notice is given to the publishers.

*An explanation of difficult words can be
found in the glossary on page 31.*

INTRODUCTION

*With their guns crackling and tyres screeching, the gangster has become one of cinema's coolest villains. Ever since his first film appearance during the **Great Depression**, the screen gangster, in pin-striped suit and felt hat has been a fantasy hero. Gangster movies provided a cinematic escape into a life of luxury, adventure and crime. Crafted out of the sensational exploits of real-life gangsters like Al Capone, John Dillinger and 'Baby Face' Nelson, the gangster movie depicted the nightmare of cities overrun with shoot-outs, massacres and gang killings. In 1934 **censorship** stopped the Hollywood film studios from making heroes out of gangsters as they were thought to be too violent. The studios turned to police films instead, creating hardened cops, as tough and cynical as the gangsters had been. These cops were determined to track down cinema's trickiest villains.*

THE UNDERWORLD

*Born and bred in the grimy alleyways and smoke-filled bars of **skid row**, for some the only escape from the gutter is the violent, criminal world of the gangster.*

LOWLIVES

Exposing the sleazy underside of New York, *The Musketeers of Pig Alley* (1912) launched the gangster

FRITZ LANG

Fritz Lang was a key figure in German cinema, directing films such as Métropolis *(1927) and* M *(1931). Lang fled Hitler's Nazi Germany in the 1930s. He ended up in the United States, where he made crime films such as* Scarlet Street *(1945).*

THE MUSKETEERS OF PIG ALLEY (1912)

One of the first movies to depict gangsters and organised crime, D.W. Griffith's silent film exposed the violent crimes committed on the streets of New York.

movie with its shoot-outs, heists and police corruption. The film *Smart Money* (1931) shows the descent from gambling into crime, while *Underworld* (1926) and *Dr Mabuse, the Gambler* (1922) focus on organized crime. The latter is about a hypnotist manipulating **hoodlums** and corrupt politicians into carrying out a huge robbery.

M (1931)

Based on the true story of serial murders that took place in Düsseldorf in Germany, M portrays a city in fear of a child killer. Despite a full-scale investigation by the police, the murderer has not been found. This disturbs members of the criminal underground who decide to hunt down the child murderer themselves. Using real criminals, M shows the cooperation between underworld gangsters and the police for the good of society, in order to catch a murderer. The film was originally entitled 'The Murderers are Among Us'.

GOING UNDER

Later American thrillers concentrated on portraying wronged men instead of straight criminals. In *Underworld USA* (1960) a boy vows revenge when his father is beaten to death and in *On the Waterfront* (1954)

GET CARTER (1971)

Get Carter is a classic British gangster film, showing the ruthlessness of the criminal underworld, as a brutal gangster seeks revenge for his brother's murder.

Marlon Brando plays a dock worker who witnesses a murder, and later exposes a dockside crime ring. British gangster movies also focus on betrayal and revenge in films such as *Get Carter* (1971), starring Michael Caine, the unusual comedy *Lock Stock and Two Smoking Barrels* (1998) and the ultra-violent *Gangster No. 1* (2000).

BRIGHTON ROCK (1947)

Based on the novel by Graham Greene, Brighton Rock is about a teenage hoodlum who loses control of his gang when he gives orders to kill a rival mobster.

GANGS OF NEW YORK (2002)

Set in the 1860s, Gangs of New York depicts the conflict between white Anglo-Saxons and Irish immigrants in New York's violent five points area. Martin Scorsese's epic film has all the crime and corruption of his gangster movies such as Goodfellas *(1990).*

OLD-TIME GANGSTERS

In 1930s America, as mobster shoot-outs hit the front pages of the newspapers, and as sound came to the cinemas, the gangster movie soared in popularity, firing up audiences with its fast cars and rattling machine guns.

LITTLE CAESAR (1930)

Loosely based on the rise and fall of Salvatore Cardinella, Little Caesar starred Edward G. Robinson as a violent and power-hungry Chicago gangster.

HOWARD HAWKS

*One of Hollywood's most popular directors, Howard Hawks directed films of many **genres** from the gangster movie Scarface (1932), to comedies such as Bringing Up Baby (1938), **film noirs** like The Big Sleep (1946) and westerns such as Rio Bravo (1959).*

HEROES...

More realistic and more exciting, the gangster **talkie** created stories out of real events. *Little Caesar* (1930) portrays the life of a violent gangster, determined to become the big boss. Similarly, *The Public Enemy* (1931) depicts the brutality of gangsters, with the famous scene of a gangster pushing a grapefruit into his lover's face.

SCARFACE (1932)

*With graphic violence, Scarface follows the bloody rise to power of Tony Camonte, who takes over the **mob**'s secretive business in illegal alcohol, after killing off the gang boss Big Louis Costillo. Ordering the massacre of rival liquor runners, Camonte shoots his way to the top of Chicago's underworld. Loosely based on the life of the real gangster Al Capone, nicknamed 'Scarface', the film recreated real-life events like the St Valentine's Day Massacre of 1929 when members of one gang were violently murdered by another gang.*

THE ROARING TWENTIES (1939)

*The Roaring Twenties depicts war veteran George Hally's new career as an illegal liquor runner. After **Prohibition** ends and alcohol is made legal again, Hally becomes an alcoholic.*

...AND ANTI-HEROES

In *Angels with Dirty Faces* (1938), a gangster who is about to be executed pretends to be a coward in order to save the children who admire him from becoming criminals themselves. The gangster hero is also undermined in *The Last Gangster* (1945) where mobsters are portrayed as ruthless and evil.

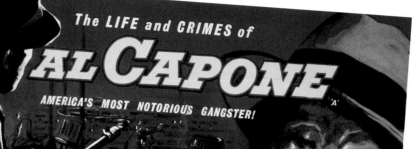

The LIFE and CRIMES of
AL CAPONE
AMERICA'S MOST NOTORIOUS GANGSTER!

Starring
ROD STEIGER
Co-Starring FAY SPAIN   JAMES GREGORY   MARTIN BALSAM
NEHEMIAH PERSOFF
AN ALLIED ARTISTS PICTURE   Distributed by Associated British Pathe

AL CAPONE (1959)

This gritty portrait of 1920s Chicago depicts the rise to power of Al Capone, the notorious American gangster, as he leaves a trail of betrayal, blackmail, and murder behind him.

THE ST VALENTINE'S DAY MASSACRE (1967)

Directed by Roger Corman, this gangster movie is a historical reconstruction of the St Valentine's Day Massacre. The actors even 'die' in the same positions as the real crime photos.

THE MOB

*Unlike the machine gun heroes of gangster movies in the thirties, a new kind of **mob** movie emerged in the 1950s exposing organized crime and corrupt politicians.*

THE CARTEL

Uncovering the dark world of mob families and crime rings, films such as *The Big Combo* (1955), examine the brutal ruthlessness of cartels, organizations carrying out corruption and murder using the rules of business. In the same way, *New York Confidential* (1955) focuses on the vulnerability of the gangster, who may be murdered simply for the good of the cartel.

SALVATORE GIULIANO (1961)

Salvatore Giuliano is a documentary style film about Sicily's notorious Mafia, an international criminal organization. It depicts a group of criminals who become heroes by fighting for Sicily's independence from Italy.

ONCE UPON A TIME IN AMERICA (1984)

*With its beautiful **cinematography** and music by Ennio Morricone, director Sergio Leone's film, Once Upon a Time in America is a portrait of four Jewish gangsters from New York's Lower East Side, dating from the beginning of the 20th century, to its decline in the 1960s.*

MARTIN SCORSESE

Arguably one of Hollywood's greatest living directors, Martin Scorsese has created some of the finest modern films to examine American society. Robert De Niro has starred in many of Scorsese's masterpieces, such as Mean Streets *(1973),* Taxi Driver *(1976),* Raging Bull *(1980) and* Goodfellas *(1990). Despite his numerous films, Scorsese is still to win an Oscar.*

GOODFELLAS (1990)

Based on a true story, Goodfellas *depicts the rise and fall of Irish-Italian mobster Henry Hill, as he makes it big through his involvement with one of New York's most powerful Mafia families.*

DIRTY BUSINESS

While modern gangster movies such as *Goodfellas* (1990) deal mainly with the brutality of the ruthless mob, Martin Scorsese's film *Casino* (1995) exposes violent, mob-run casinos in Las Vegas. *Donnie Brasco* (1997), on the other hand, focuses on the human side of the mob, when an undercover cop, Johnny Depp, is accepted into the tight-knit community of the Mafia.

THE GODFATHER (1972)

Adapted from the novel by Mario Puzo and starring Marlon Brando and Al Pacino, The Godfather *follows the story of Michael, son of the Mafia boss and 'godfather', Don Vito Corleone. Michael refuses to enter his father's ruthless business of gambling and prostitution. But when rival gangsters attempt to kill the godfather, Michael is dragged deeper and deeper into a violent cycle of revenge. Director Francis Ford Coppola made two further Godfather films in 1974 and 1990.*

CARLITO'S WAY (1993)

Depicting a former drug-dealer trying to go straight, Carlito's Way *tells the tragic tale of a man sucked back into his criminal past. Ultimately, the film exposes the government as the most corrupt criminal of all.*

MODERN-DAY HOODS

Focusing on betrayal and deception within the parallel worlds of organized crime and the police force, modern gangster movies often portray a world turned upside down, full of police spies, called moles, and undercover gangsters.

EASTERN INFLUENCE

Quentin Tarantino's film *Reservoir Dogs* (1992) examines the notion of honour among thieves. Six strangers, who team up to carry out a diamond robbery, discover there is a mole in their group, and start suspecting each other. Tarantino's film pays tribute to Hong Kong gangster films, borrowing from movies such as John Woo's *A Better Tomorrow II* (1987) and *City on Fire* (1987).

MEAN STREETS (1973)

Martin Scorsese's breakthrough film Mean Streets *is a realistic look at gangsters in the New York area called Little Italy, trying to combine pressures of the Mafia and religion.*

TAKESHI KITANO

Renowned film-maker and actor Takeshi Kitano specializes in offbeat gangster movies such as Violent Cop *(1989) and* Zatoichi *(2003). Kitano also works as a TV presenter and comedian in Japan, under his alias 'Beat Takeshi'.*

RESERVOIR DOGS (1992)

Quentin Tarantino's film combines humour, sharp dialogue and popular culture with many references to other crime films, such as the colour-coded criminals in The Taking of Pelham One Two Three *(1974).*

HARD BOILED (1992)

Set in Hong Kong, Hard Boiled follows rebel cop Tequila who teams up with undercover detective Tony, after his partner is killed in a raid on a gun-smuggling Triad, an underground criminal ring in Hong Kong. John Woo's earlier films have been criticised for glamorising gangsters. In Hard Boiled he glamorises the police, depicting tough cops and brutal gun battles. Hard Boiled was Woo's last Hong Kong action film before he began making films in Hollywood.

PULP FICTION (1994)

Unusual in its depiction of foolish gangsters, Pulp Fiction tells of hopeless crooks and soul-searching hit-men, trying to survive in the underworld of organized crime.

YAKUZAS AND TRIADS

Films such as *Infernal Affairs* (2002) expose the crooked morals of the Hong Kong police, who use the same tactics as the Triad gangsters by planting a mole undercover. In Tikeshi Yitano's comedic thriller *Sonatine* (1993), a betrayed gangster seeks revenge, and in *Brother* (2001) a violent yakuza tries to set up a drug racket in Los Angeles.

INFERNAL AFFAIRS (2002)

*A stylish **mob** thriller about organized crime in Hong Kong, Infernal Affairs focuses on an undercover cop in the Triad crime ring and a mole in the police force, as each is given the task to seek the other out.*

Outlaws

*The exploits of criminals made sensational news stories during the **Great Depression** in the United States. This made heroes out of public enemies like John Dillinger, Bonnie and Clyde and Ma Barker, who all looted stores and gas stations.*

Gun Crazy (1949)

In Joseph H. Lewis' Gun Crazy a gun-loving man is led astray by a greedy and violent woman. Leaving behind a trail of robberies, the doomed lovers show how dangerous guns can be in the wrong hands.

On the Run

The **film noir** *Gun Crazy* (1949) was originally released as *Deadly is the Female*. It follows a man under the spell of a gun-wielding woman, anticipating the allure of the real-life Bonnie and Clyde. French gangster movies like *L'Ascenseur Pour L'Echafaud* (1957) paid tribute to Hollywood gangster movies. It features two lovers on the run, a murdered husband and a jazz score by musician Miles Davis.

Breathless (1960)

Jean Luc Godard's masterpiece of French cinema combines gangsters, philosophy and French 1960s glamour. Breathless tells the story of petty criminal Jesse's attempt to escape the police.

The Real-Life Bonnie and Clyde

Bonnie Parker and Clyde Barrow were notorious criminals, who robbed gas stations and banks during the Great Depression. In 1934, after a string of robberies and murders, the fugitive couple were caught close to their hideout in Louisiana, USA. They were turned into celebrities when Bonnie's poem detailing their escapades was published.

BONNIE AND CLYDE (1967)

Set during the Great Depression, Bonnie and Clyde *follows Bonnie, a bored farm-girl desperate for love and adventure, and amateur bank robber Clyde, on a crime spree through the United States. Arthur Penn's film, with its beautiful* **cinematography***, is criticised for portraying gangsters as romantic heroes rather than violent killers, even though the film broke new ground in its graphic depiction of violence.*

THE GETAWAY (1972)

Sam Peckinpah's The Getaway *is a thriller about a professional safe-cracker, caught in a web of deception, betrayal and revenge after being freed from prison. Forced into another bank robbery, he has to outwit his partners and the police in order to keep his freedom.*

KILLING SPREES

The French film *Plein Soleil* (1960) depicts a man seduced by the idea of a glamorous lifestyle, causing him to commit murder. A similar trail of violence is left by women on the run in the groundbreaking *Thelma and Louise* (1991), when two women decide to escape their unhappy lives and marriages. After Louise kills a man who attacks Thelma, the women head for Mexico, to escape the police and the death penalty.

NATURAL BORN KILLERS (1994)

Natural Born Killers *tells of two lovers, Mickey and Mallory, on a killing spree. As they are turned into TV celebrities, Oliver Stone's film examines the media's portrayal of violence.*

THIEVES

Despite early movies like The Great Train Robbery *(1903) and* The Bold Bank Robbery *(1905), the crime film with its cool crooks reached its peak in the 1950s.*

THE STICK-UP

With its complex plots and stylish villains, the heist or caper movie was inspired by John Huston's film noir *The Asphalt Jungle* (1950). French gangsters attempted jewel robberies in *Touchez-pas au Grisbi* (1954) and *Du Rififi Chez Les Hommes* (1954), in which there is a 32-minute robbery scene, carried out in complete silence.

HEIST (2001)

With its complicated plot full of unexpected twists, Heist *follows a gang of criminals planning a robbery on a shipment of gold. The thieves come up with numerous scheming ways of keeping the loot for themselves.*

HIGH SIERRA (1941)

With a gangster hero who has broken out of prison to take part in one last jewel robbery, High Sierra *is a **film noir** in which actor Humphrey Bogart (right) plays Earle, a professional gangster with a heart of gold who is forced to go on the run when the robbery goes wrong.*

JOHN HUSTON

Beginning his career as a screenwriter for the Warner Bros studio, Huston wrote scripts, adapted from plays and novels, such as the Oscar-nominated Dr Ehrlich's Magic Bullet *(1940) and* High Sierra *(1941). He was then given* The Maltese Falcon *(1941) to direct, now considered to be the ultimate private detective movie. Huston directed several classic films, including* The Treasure of the Sierra Madre *(1948).*

THE ASPHALT JUNGLE (1950)

*One of the first **caper** movies, The Asphalt Jungle depicts a gang of crooks planning a diamond robbery. Among them are 'Doc', the brains behind the burglary, safe-cracker Louis, getaway driver Gus, muscle man Dix and money man Emmerich. Despite careful planning, the job goes wrong and the thieves have to make a getaway. One of the first great caper movies, John Huston's film created criminals who were not simply villains. Rather than being caught by the police, it is their own character flaws that cause their downfall. The Asphalt Jungle is in the style of film noir, set in the dark and grimy underworld of the city.*

GETTING AWAY WITH IT

The heist movie often sees crooks running off with the loot, before the double-crossing and corruption begins. In Stanley Kubrick's *The Killing* (1956), which inspired Tarantino's *Reservoir Dogs* (1992), a gang of thieves steal $200,000 from a racecourse, before they start trying to outdo each other. In *$* (1971) a bank clerk steals the loot from the robbers' safety deposit boxes, while in *The Italian Job* (1969) the crooks nearly get away with the gold, until the ground is literally swept from beneath their feet in a famous car chase across the Alps.

BOB LE FLAMBEUR (1956)

Featuring fancy cars and sharp-suited gangsters, Bob le Flambeur pays tribute to the Hollywood gangster movies of the 1930s. This film tells the tale of a casino robbery by a gang of professional thieves.

OCEAN'S ELEVEN (2001)

A remake of the caper movie with Frank Sinatra and Dean Martin, Ocean's Eleven (2001) follows a large gang of professional crooks as they plan a heist on three Las Vegas casinos.

ASSASSINS

Hired hit-men have been killing off victims since the gangster film began. But the professional assassin, solitary and methodical, became popular when political assassinations were taking place during the **Cold War**.

IN COLD BLOOD

While contract killers have long been part of the gangster's **mob** in thrillers like *The Killers* (1946), where two hit-men hunt down a former gangster, the assassin made it big in *This Gun For Hire* (1942). A cool and calculating killer, the hit-man became cinema's favourite criminal. The movies *Le Samouraï* (1967) and *The Day of the Jackal* (1973) focus on the ruthless efficiency and cold determination of the gunman, carefully planning a murder while cleverly evading the police.

THIS GUN FOR HIRE (1942)

*Adapted from a novel by Graham Greene, this **film noir** set the tone for the solitary assassin. Living alone in a rented room, the assassin of* This Gun For Hire *is a ruthless killer, who cares for nobody but a stray cat.*

QUENTIN TARANTINO

Tarantino shot to the top of the film world when he wrote and directed Reservoir Dogs *(1992), and wrote* True Romance *(1993) and* Natural Born Killers *(1994). With sharp dialogue and an unusual sequencing of events, his later films such as* Pulp Fiction *(1994) and* Kill Bill *(2003 & 2004) are often violent, blood-drenched movies.*

LE SAMOURAÏ (1967)

Jean Pierre Melville's tribute to the American gangster movie, Le Samouraï *examines the lonely existence and mental breakdown of a cold-blooded hit-man.*

LONE KILLERS

Focusing on the solitary and emotionless assassin, Luc Besson's *Léon* (1994) is about a hit-man who learns to love and to live when he makes friends with an orphaned young girl. The hired killer in *Ghost Dog: The Way of the Samurai* (1999) lives a life according to the Samurai's code, until his employers decide to get rid of him.

LA FEMME NIKITA (1990)

In Luc Besson's stylish but very violent thriller, a drug addict is trained as a female assassin, after she is charged with murder.

GROSSE POINT BLANK (1997)

A crime comedy, Grosse Pointe Blank follows Martin Blank, a professional hit-man on a losing streak. Having failed in his previous contracts, he returns to his home town of Grosse Pointe on a job, and to attend his ten-year high school reunion. A mix of black comedy and high school romance, the killer in Grosse Pointe Blank is a real human being in conflict, as he questions the morality of being a hit-man.

KILL BILL (2003 & 2004)

A tribute to Chinese martial arts films (called 'wuxia') with their gravity-defying fights and mystical killing powers, Tarantino's Kill Bill see Uma Thurman as 'The Bride', a former member of the Deadly Viper Assassination Squad, hell-bent on revenge.

BAD COP

As time went on, the hardened criminal-catcher evolved into the dishonest cop. On a mission to rid the streets of crooks by whatever means, police departments became overrun with bad cops, bribery and corruption.

SERPICO (1973)

Based on a true story, Serpico exposes corruption in the New York Police Department, as cop Serpico takes on the real criminals – the corrupt police officers.

PRINCE OF THE CITY (1981)

In Prince of the City, the New York police are depicted as a corrupt department. When a cop blows the whistle on his colleagues' illegal doings, the world around him comes crashing down.

THE ROTTEN BARREL

Corrupt police have replaced violent gangsters and thieves as cinema's worst villains since Sidney Lumet's film *Serpico* (1973), in which cops make money out of criminals. The police are portrayed as brutal and corrupt in modern films too, with police breaking the law in order to catch criminals. In *Exit Wounds* (2001) the police deal in heroin, while in *Training Day* (2001) an idealistic new recruit is made to question the brutality and dishonest tactics of his out-of-control superior officer.

DARK BLUE (2002)

Dark Blue is set in 1992, when Los Angeles was awaiting a verdict in the case of white police officers accused of beating black motorist Rodney King. It examines police intimidation and corruption.

L.A. CONFIDENTIAL (1997)

Set in 1950s Los Angeles, L.A. Confidential *traces three cops through a series of gangster killings, Hollywood sleaze and police corruption. Learning to work together, they combine brains and brawn to get to the bottom of L.A.'s criminal underworld.*

THE HAT SQUAD

More like gangsters than police detectives, the hat squad was a real-life gang of cops in 1950s Los Angeles. They dressed like gangsters, wearing felt hats called fedoras. Hunting down murderers and thieves, they were not afraid to break the law, or even a bone or two, in order to catch the criminals.

LOOSE CANNONS

Ever since *The Big Heat* (1953), in which a cop turns to the dark side of the law to take revenge on **mob** murderers, the rogue cop has been key to the police thriller. Tough cops beyond the law, like the alcoholic and racist detective played by Gene Hackman in *The French Connection* (1971) and the tough vigilante in *Dirty Harry* (1970), bend the rules to catch the criminals any way they can.

DIRTY HARRY (1970)

The original outsider cop, Dirty Harry is a tough, heavy-handed detective determined to catch a serial killer in San Francisco, USA.

NARC (2002)

With a hand-held camera conveying the harsh reality of cops on the street, Narc *follows two undercover narcotics (drugs) police officers trying to solve the death of a fellow 'narc'.*

PRIVATE EYES

*Fast-talking, cynical private detectives were popular **film noir** heroes. Unlike gangster-catching cops, these shady private eyes investigated the sleazier side of modern life such as blackmail and betrayal.*

FILM NOIR

Film noir is a cinematic style, which is often filmed in black and white and in urban locations to create a world of crime and betrayal. Famous film noirs include Double Indemnity *(1944) and* Laura *(1944).*

HARD BOILED

In *The Maltese Falcon* (1941) a cynical private eye is lured into a web of intrigue and betrayal by a deceitful woman. *Murder My Sweet* (1944) depicts a private eye who is only looking out for himself, and in *Laura* (1944) there is a new twist when the detective falls in love with a female murder victim.

THE BIG SLEEP (1946)

In this tense film noir, a wealthy man hires private eye, Philip Marlowe, to discover why his youngest daughter Carmen is being blackmailed. Tracing the blackmailer to his own home, Marlowe finds him murdered and thus becomes entangled in a web of crime and corruption. Famous for its intricate plot, The Big Sleep is adapted from a Raymond Chandler novel. But it is the stylish, dark and threatening atmosphere, and the onscreen tension between actors Humphrey Bogart and Lauren Bacall, that make The Big Sleep a classic.

KISS ME DEADLY (1955)

A film noir thriller, Kiss Me Deadly is about a poor and shabby private eye, dragged into a web of corruption by a hitchhiker who is brutally murdered.

NOT SO TOUGH

At the end of the film noir era, Orson Welles' *Touch of Evil* (1958) has a more political edge, with Charlton Heston playing a Mexican policeman, caught up in drug smuggling and police corruption in a town on the Mexican border. Alfred Hitchcock's masterpiece *Vertigo* (1958) focuses on the breakdown of an ex-police officer turned private detective, who becomes obsessed with the beautiful woman he is hired to follow.

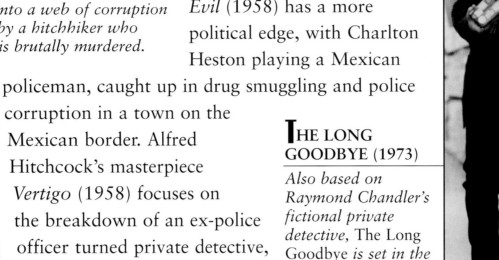

THE LONG GOODBYE (1973)

Also based on Raymond Chandler's fictional private detective, The Long Goodbye is set in the 1970s, and focuses on a detective who is out of touch with the corrupt modern world (right).

CHINATOWN (1974)

Set in 1930s L.A., Jack Nicholson plays private eye Jake Gittes, who becomes involved in a corporate conspiracy when he starts investigating a husband's betrayal of his wife. A tribute to film noir, Chinatown updates the detective film, with Jake, a scarred ex-cop hiding from his past.

THE BIG LEBOWSKI (1998)

A variation on The Big Sleep *(1946), the Coen Brothers' film* The Big Lebowski *follows bowling fanatic 'The Dude', who is mistaken by mobsters for an L.A. millionaire.*

SLEUTHS

Whether investigating murders in the foggy, gas-lit streets of Victorian London or the social circles of 1930s upper-class society, the amateur sleuth (detective) has outwitted criminals and audiences.

IT'S ELEMENTARY!

Sherlock Holmes, the professional sleuth, is one of cinema's most filmed characters, with over 200 appearances. The most popular incarnation of this master of disguise was Basil Rathbone as Holmes in *The Hound of the Baskervilles* (1939).

THE PEARL OF DEATH (1944)

Based on The Adventure of the Six Napoleons, by Arthur Conan Doyle, The Pearl of Death depicts Sherlock Holmes in pursuit of a cursed pearl and a monster.

THE ADVENTURES OF SHERLOCK HOLMES (1939)

Arch-villain Professor Moriarty sets out to destroy Holmes' reputation by devising a series of mysterious murders to keep the gentleman detective busy, while he steals the crown jewels.

The
Adventures of
SHERLOCK
HOLMES

RATHBONE NIGEL BRUCE
IDA LUPINO ALAN MARSHAL
AND TERRY KILBURN GEORGE ZUCCO
HENRY STEPHENSON E. E. CLIVE

THE THIN MAN (1934)

A comic murder mystery, The Thin Man *follows a newlywed couple who step in to solve a murder when the police prove unable to. With clever conversation and a cocktail or two, the amateur detectives expose the murderer over dinner.*

TALENTED AMATEURS

In many films, ordinary people wrongly suspected of murder sometimes make the best detectives, often risking their lives to clear their name. In *The Blue Dahlia* (1946) and *The Fugitive* (1993), starring Harrison Ford, a man must find his wife's killer before the police catch up with him. Hitchcock also turned innocent suspects into heroes in films like *The 39 Steps* (1935), where a man investigates the murder of a woman, hunted down by spies. The murder mystery has also created many popular sleuths like Agatha Christie's detective character Hercule Poirot, who is on the trail of a millionaire's killer in *Murder on the Orient Express* (1974).

DASHIEL HAMMETT

Born in 1894, Dashiel Hammett was an American writer, who created hardened, wise-cracking detectives such as Sam Spade in The Maltese Falcon *(1941) and the crime-busting couple in* The Thin Man *(1934), who solve murders for the sheer excitement of it.*

THE PRIVATE LIFE OF SHERLOCK HOLMES (1970)

Directed by comic genius Billy Wilder, The Private Life of Sherlock Holmes *sees Holmes and Dr Watson on the case of a Belgian woman's missing husband. While falling for the beautiful Belgian, Holmes uncovers a plot involving a troupe of midgets, Queen Victoria and the Loch Ness Monster. A humorous look at the Sherlock Holmes myth,* The Private Life of Sherlock Holmes *adds a human touch to the lives of Holmes and Watson.*

AGATHA CHRISTIE'S
DEATH ON THE NILE

A murderer strikes on board the luxury Nile steamer *Karnak* – and Hercule Poirot faces his most baffling case.

DEATH ON THE NILE (1978)

Based on one of Agatha Christie's most famous novels, Death on the Nile *features an all-star cast, as Belgian sleuth Hercule Poirot investigates the death of a wealthy woman, murdered on board a luxury steam boat cruising down the Nile in Egypt.*

CRIME VICTIMS

CWhile most crime films focus on criminals and detectives, suspense thrillers concentrate on the victims of crime. Trying to escape a crazed killer, or to clear their name of a murder they did not commit, the victim in danger keeps viewers on the edge of their seats.

HOME ALONE

The fear of being attacked at home started with *The Lonely Villa* (1909), in which a group of robbers break into a house, threatening a man's wife and children. *Funny Games* (1997) and *Panic Room* (2002) also give violent portraits of families held hostage in their own homes. Similarly, movies like *Pacific Heights* (1990) or *Cold Creek Manor* (2003) show a family's dream home and lifestyle come crashing down because of a crazed killer.

DAVID FINCHER

Starting out as an animator for the special effects company Industrial Light & Magic, Fincher then founded his own production company, Propaganda Films. He directed the most expensive debut feature, Alien 3 *(1992). His films include* Se7en *(1995),* Fight Club *(1999) and* Panic Room *(2002), featuring his dark* **cinematography** *and unusual camerawork.*

SCARLET STREET (1945)

A remake of Jean Renoir's La Chienne *(1931),* Scarlet Street *is a tale of obsession, betrayal and murder. When Chris Cross becomes the victim of gold-digging couple 'Lazy Legs' and her boyfriend Johnny, he carries out a terrifying act of revenge.*

PANIC ROOM (2002)

David Fincher's film Panic Room *focuses on a mother and daughter trapped inside their house in Manhattan in New York, when three burglars break in, searching for a hidden stash of money. The mother and daughter escape to the panic room, a secret room protected by a steel door, a security alarm and a phone. They try to signal for help, but in the end they have to fight for their own survival. With its sleek cinematography and tense atmosphere,* Panic Room *is a thriller full of suspense. Fincher also uses advanced filming techniques to stylishly zoom through objects.*

RUNNING SCARED

In many crime films the victims are trying to escape and outwit their tormentors. Valets and nannies terrorise their employers in *The Servant* (1963) and *The Hand that Rocks the Cradle* (1992), while a husband's one night stand with a woman who is not his wife leads to disaster in *Fatal Attraction* (1987). In *Sleeping With the Enemy* (1991) a woman beaten by her husband must change her identity to escape him, while in *Misery* (1990) there is no escape for novelist Paul Sheldon, trapped inside the house of his 'number one fan' after he is injured in a car accident.

CAPE FEAR (1991)

Martin Scorsese's remake of Cape Fear *(1962) is the story of the violent Max Cady, hell-bent on taking revenge on Sam Bowden, the lawyer who put him in jail by concealing evidence that could have helped his case. Cady sends three thugs to beat Bowden up, forcing Bowden and his family to face their past.*

RANSOM (1996)

A cop-turned-bad action thriller, Ransom *stars Mel Gibson as a self-made millionaire, whose son is kidnapped. When the ransom drop goes wrong, he takes the matter into his own hands.*

FILM TECHNOLOGY

FILMING BULLET HITS

Bullet wounds are created by fixing false bullet holes, made of latex, on to an actor's skin, before adding make-up and fake blood to make it look more realistic. To create the impression of a bullet hit, an air gun is sometimes used, which fires soft gelatine capsules, filled with fake blood, at an actor.

FIRING SQUIBS

Small explosives, called squibs, are also used to create the impression of bullet fire. The squib is attached to a protective metal plate, which is fixed to the actor's body. A bag of fake blood is placed over the top to explode on impact, when the squib is set off from the control panel.

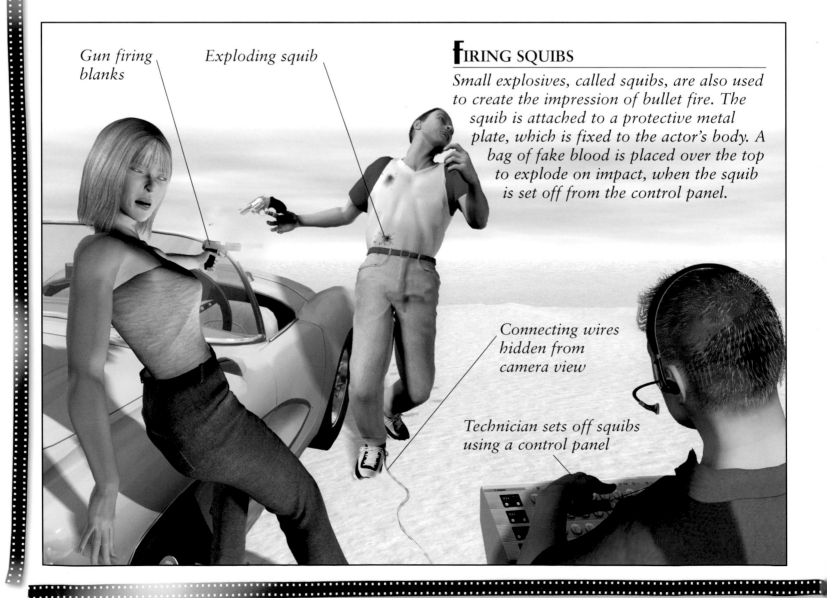

Gun firing blanks

Exploding squib

Connecting wires hidden from camera view

Technician sets off squibs using a control panel

GLOSSARY

caper
light–hearted or dishonest activity

censorship
banning of anything considered offensive, or a threat to security

cinematography
art of photography and camera work in films

Cold War
state of hostility between nations without an actual war. The term usually describes the situation between the Soviet Union and United States between 1945 and the late 1960s.

film noir
film genre associated with violence and crime. Films are often set in the darkness of night with rainy streets.

genre
style or category of film, literature or art

Great Depression
economic crisis in the United States that began with the stock market crash of 1929 and continued through the 1930s

Hays Production Code
code that outlined general standards of good taste and ruled on what could and could not be shown in U.S. films. It was created in 1930 and enforced from 1934 onwards.

hoodlum
violent person, especially one who is a member of a group of criminals

The Mob
another term used to describe the Mafia

Prohibition
prevention by law of the manufacture and sale of alcohol in the United States from 1920 to 1933

skid row
run-down part of a town where homeless people and alcoholics live

talkie
film with sound

INDEX